Play with Triangles

Patchwork Designs & Projects

by

Bonnie K. Browning & Phyllis D. Miller

American Quilter's Society
P. O. Box 3290 • Paducah, KY 42002-3290

Located in Paducah, Kentucky, the American Quilter's Society (AQS) is dedicated to promoting the accomplishments of today's quilters. Through its publications and events, AQS strives to honor today's quiltmakers and their work and to inspire future creativity and innovation in quiltmaking.

EDITOR: CHERRY PYRON
BOOK DESIGN/ILLUSTRATIONS: ELAINE WILSON
COVER DESIGN: MICHAEL BUCKINGHAM
PHOTOGRAPHY: CHARLES R. LYNCH

Library of Congress Cataloging-in-Publication Data
Browning, Bonnie K.
     Play with triangles / Bonnie K. Browning & Phyllis D. Miller
     p.   cm.
     ISBN 1-57432-753-4
     1. Quilt--Patterns.   2. Half-square triangles.   3. Rotary Cutting
     I. Title.
TT835.S42 2000
746.46041--dc21   Applied for
                                       CIP

Additional copies of this book may be ordered from the American Quilter's Society, PO Box 3290, Paducah, KY 42002-3290.

Contents

Introduction

Many quilt patterns use triangles as an element of the design. The bias lines created by dividing squares into triangles add motion and an opportunity to use color in exciting combinations.

Today's methods of quiltmaking make it easy to work with the bias edges of the triangles. Using rotary cutting tools and sewing the triangles in squares or grids are ways to reduce the possibility of stretching bias edges. The sewing is done before cutting along the bias edges.

In this book, you will find 32 designs and 7 projects in which to play with triangles. The designs can be sewn in two colors of fabric, multiple colors, or using scraps. We prefer to sew half-square triangles in blocks, eliminating the need to cut and work with any bias edges. For scrappy designs made entirely of triangles, the half-square method is our choice. If you need to make many triangles using two fabrics, try the grid method.

For each design, the block size and cutting requirements are provided. You can make these blocks in any size by changing the cutting size of the squares. To help you determine the amount of fabric you need to make your quilt, we provide a chart giving the number of squares that can be cut from yardage.

We've had fun gathering and stitching quilts to show you a variety of patterns and color schemes. Use these ideas to make your own quilts or use the ideas as stepping stones to have fun playing with triangles.

Bonnie & Phyllis

Triangles

*F*our methods are presented to cut and sew triangles. One of these methods is the corner-square technique that can save lots of time since you only cut squares before sewing. Any of these methods can be used for the projects; it is usually easier and more accurate to work with squares or the grid methods than working with the bias edges of cut triangles.

Seam allowances (¼") are included in the cutting measurements for each method.

The advantages and disadvantages of each method are outlined. Give each method a try and see which you prefer. For projects which require a large number of different fabrics, the square method is fast and efficient. When the number of fabrics is fewer, the grid method might be more practical to use.

Cutting measurements are outlined for each of the methods. In addition, a Quick Reference Chart is included for squares that finish in inches and half-inches. You can change the size of any of the blocks by changing the sizes of the triangle or half-squares and plain blocks.

INDIVIDUAL TRIANGLES

Advantage: Every triangle can be a different fabric (see SOUTHERN CHARM on page 28).

Disadvantage: Bias edges must be sewn together. Care must be taken not to stretch the bias edges during sewing and pressing.

Cutting Measurements: Cut squares the finished dimension of the short side of the

finished triangle + ⅞". Cut the square in half to make two individual triangles (Fig. 1).

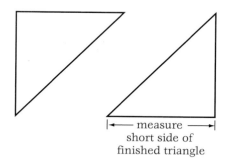

|← measure →|
short side of
finished triangle

Fig. 1. Two individual triangles
size = finished size of short side + ⅞"

HALF-SQUARES METHOD

Advantage: Sewing bias edges is eliminated, resulting in greater accuracy. This method is good to use when making scrap quilts or quilts that have several fabrics. Save squares from your quilting projects and periodically sew them into half-squares. Before you know it, you will have enough to make a new quilt. Chain piecing (see page 8) can be used in this method, reducing the amount of time required to sew the squares.

Disadvantage: When sewing a variety of fabrics together where the thread count and tightness of the weave vary, you might find that the edges will not line up exactly. If you are using many different fabric weaves, cut the squares ¼" larger and trim the half-squares to the finished size plus ½" seam allowances after they are sewn.

Cutting Measurements: Cut squares the

finished size of the desired square + ⅞". Draw a diagonal from lower left corner to upper right corner on a light square. Place the light square with the drawn line, right sides together, with another square. Sew ¼" on both sides of the drawn line (Fig. 2). Cut the triangles apart on the drawn line. Press the half-squares open. Each set of two squares results in two identical half-squares.

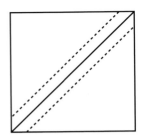

Fig. 2. Half-squares method
size = finished size + ⅞"
draw diagonal line and sew ¼" on each side of drawn line

GRID METHOD

Advantage: By marking a grid on the wrong side of one fabric and placing it right sides together with another fabric, you can create many uniform half-squares in a limited amount of time. Because the sewing is done before the triangles are cut apart, the half-squares are accurate and stretching of the bias edges is prevented.

Disadvantage: To keep the squares free from distortion, care must be taken to keep the squares together and not let them "walk" as you sew. Pin the fabrics together in a few places to keep them secure.

Cutting Measurements: Determine the number of half-squares you need and divide by 2; that is the number of squares you will

need to draw on the grid. On a square of fabric, draw horizontal and vertical lines forming squares that are the finished size you need + ⅞". Draw the grid at least ¼" inside the edges of the fabric. Draw diagonal lines from upper left to lower right, crossing the corners of each square. Sew ¼" on the left side of each diagonal line; when you reach the edge of the fabric, lift the presser foot and turn the fabric around; stitch ¼" from the other side of the drawn line (Fig. 3). Continue sewing until you have stitched on both sides of each of the diagonal lines. Cut the triangles apart on each drawn line — horizontal, vertical, and diagonal. Each square on the grid makes two half-squares.

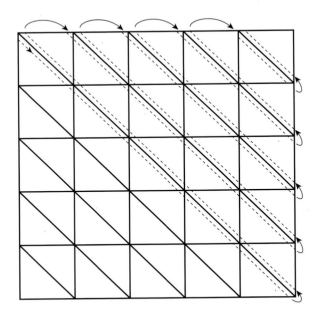

Fig. 3. Grid method
a. Draw grid lines finished width plus ⅞".
b. Draw diagonal lines from upper left to lower right.
c. Sew ¼" on both sides of diagonal lines.
d. Cut apart on all drawn lines.

BIAS STRIPS METHOD

Advantage: For this method, two bias strips are sewn together and then half-squares are cut from the sewn strip. There is little variation in the size of the half-squares. This method is especially useful for small half-squares because the seam allowances can be pressed open before the half-squares are cut.

Disadvantage: Care must be taken not to stretch the bias strips while sewing them together or while pressing the seam allowances.

Cutting Measurements: Cut the bias strips 1" wider than the finished size of the half-square. Sew the bias strips together, alternating colors. Press the seam allowances toward the dark fabric (or press open for small half-squares). Use a small acrylic ruler and rotary cutter to cut squares ½" larger than the finished size of the half-square you need (Fig. 4).

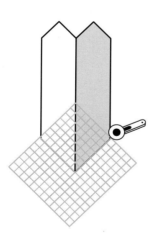

Fig. 4. Bias-strip method

CORNER-SQUARE TECHNIQUE

Many designs can be simplified by using a square to make triangles in the corners of the block. Examples of blocks that can be sewn with corner squares are Snowball (p. 16), Robbing Peter to Pay Paul (p. 16), and Bow Tie (p. 17).

Advantage: Time is saved by cutting squares for the corners instead of individual triangles. Larger squares can be cut for the background instead of cutting odd-shaped pieces. No templates are needed. The stitching line on the corner squares can be marked by pressing the square in half to make a triangle. The pressed mark becomes the seam line. It is easy to align the corner square with the corner of the background square.

Disadvantage: Some fabric is wasted by cutting off the corners ¼" from the seam line.

Cutting Measurements: The size of the squares for the corners varies, depending on the design. Sometimes the square is small (see Robbing Peter to Pay Paul, p. 16) or it can be larger (see Floating Stars, p. 23). Press a fold in the corner square to make a triangle. Place the corner square on the background square, right sides together; make sure the corners and edges line up. Sew on the fold line. Press the seam line to set the stitches. Trim the corner, leaving ¼" seam allowance from the stitching line (Fig. 5). If you want to use the waste corner for another project, sew a second seam line ½" from the first stitching line before you trim the corner.

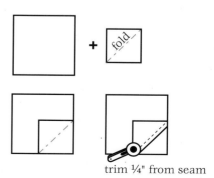

trim ¼" from seam

Fig. 5. Corner-square technique

General Instructions

CUTTING

Accuracy in cutting is very important. The use of a rotary cutter, mat, and acrylic rulers helps to make cutting more accurate and efficient.

SORTING FABRIC

If you want to make a scrap quilt, you need to sort the fabrics into light, medium, and dark values. It is the contrast between a fabric and the one next to it that delineates the design. For example, if you want a star shape to stand out, make the star in dark fabric and contrast it against a light background (see STAR IN A STAR, p. 27).

Here is an easy way to sort a pile of squares into light, medium, and dark piles. Start by sorting the squares into only two piles — a light pile and a dark pile. Look at the fabric; if it is not light, put it in the dark pile. If it does not seem to be dark, put it in the light pile.

Once you have all the squares sorted into these two piles, take the light pile and sort it again into light and dark piles. You will see that the darks of this pile are medium values.

Take the dark pile and sort it into two piles, a light pile and a dark pile. The lights in this group will also be medium values. Combine the two medium piles for the medium values.

Try this method, it takes the guesswork out of sorting the squares!

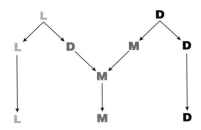

CHAIN PIECING

When you need to sew several of the same pieces together, it saves time to sew these units with a continuous row of stitching. To make half-squares, place two squares, right sides together. Sew ¼" to the left of the diagonal line drawn on the lighter square. Do not cut the threads. Pick up another set of squares and continue sewing to the left of the diagonal line. How many should you sew? It is sometimes helpful to sew enough in one group to make a block. Sewing in block groups helps you keep

---

Tips for rotary cutting

✧ Keep a sharp blade in the rotary cutter.

✧ Immediately after making a cut, close the blade guard.

✧ Always cut pushing the cutter away from your body.

✧ Do not try to cut close to or over straight pins; if you get too close, you may nick the blade.

✧ Position your hand on the ruler so your little finger is just off the edge. This will help keep the ruler from sliding as you put pressure against it while cutting.

✧ Use the same ruler to cut an entire project. The lines on another ruler may not line up the same, resulting in different sizes of pieces.

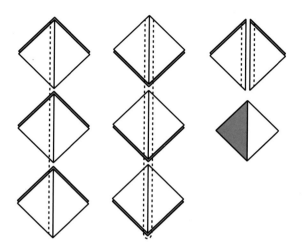

Fig. 6. Chain piecing

count of how many you have made. Once you have enough squares sewn to make one block, turn the group around and sew ¼" away from the opposite side of the drawn line (Fig. 6).

For example, in the JUDY'S XQUISITE SCRAP QUILT (page 24), you need three light/dark squares, three light/medium squares, and three medium/dark squares. If you chain piece these units together, you will have all of the pieces to make a block (this actually is enough to make two blocks since each set of squares makes two half-squares). This also saves having to sort out the half-squares again. Do not cut the chain-pieced groups apart until you are ready to sew the blocks together.

Squares from Yardage

CUT SIZE SQUARE	FAT QUARTER	¼ YD	½ YD	1 YD	1¼ YD	1½ YD	2 YD
1½"	154	140	308	644	812	980	1316
2"	90	84	168	357	462	546	735
2½"	56	48	96	224	272	336	448
3"	42	28	70	154	196	238	322
3½"	30	24	48	120	144	180	240
4"	20	20	40	80	110	130	170
4½"	16	9	27	63	81	99	135
5"	12	8	24	56	64	80	112
5½"	9	7	21	42	56	63	84
6"	9	7	14	35	49	56	77
6½"	6	6	12	30	36	48	60
7"	6	6	12	30	36	42	60
7½"	4	5	10	20	25	35	45
8"	4	5	10	20	25	30	40

To use this chart, select the cut size of the square in column one. Determine the number of squares required and follow the row across to find a number equal to or larger than the number of squares needed. The amount of fabric to buy is at the top of that column. For example: 60 3" cut squares are needed; purchase ½ yd. fabric.

If you need a square size not listed on the chart, use the next larger measurement. For example, for 2⅞" cut squares, use the 3" row.

Quick Reference Chart
for Cutting Squares

SQUARE FINISHED SIZE	HALF-SQUARE CUT SIZE	PLAIN SQUARE CUT SIZE
1"	1⅞"	1½"
1½"	2⅜"	2"
2"	2⅞"	2½"
2½"	3⅜"	3"
3"	3⅞"	3½"
3½"	4⅜"	4"
4"	4⅞"	4½"
4½"	5⅜"	5"
5"	5⅞"	5½"
5½"	6⅜"	6"
6"	6⅞"	6½"
6½"	7⅜"	7"
7"	7⅞"	7½"
7½"	8⅜"	8"
8	8⅞"	8½"
8½"	9⅜"	9"
9"	9⅞"	9½'
9½"	10⅜"	10'
10"	10⅞"	10½"
11"	11⅞"	11½"
12"	12⅞"	12½"
13"	13⅞"	13½"
14"	14⅞"	14½"

For other sizes use these formulas:

Half-squares: Finished size of square + ⅞" = cut size of square

Plain squares: Finished size of square + ½" = cut size of square

Designs

Many designs use triangles. Once you have made half-squares (two triangles sewn into a square), you can begin to sew them into blocks. The designs are divided into several categories: triangles only, corner-square blocks, triangles combined with squares, and two sizes of triangles. Browse through this section before you begin playing with triangles. Feel free to change the color schemes.

TRIANGLES ONLY

Just Triangles

by Mary Sowell

Lay out the half-squares and let the color of the triangles create a design that is asymmetrical. Mary Sowell used rectangles to make the border, with half-squares in each corner.

BLOCK STYLE: Half-squares

FINISHED BLOCK SIZE: 2"

cut 2⅞" squares for half-squares

border #1: 1", cut 1⅜ strips

border #2: 2¼" pieced rectangles are
1" x 2¼", cut 1½" x 2¾"

Not Just Any Old Barn Raising

by Mary Sowell

Lay out the half-squares in an organized fashion to create a barn-raising setting. Two borders frame the quilt; a plain solid strip separates the center from the border of pieced squares. Notice that the fabrics are identical to those used in Just Triangles. Mary used one set of half-squares in each quilt.

BLOCK STYLE: Half-squares

FINISHED BLOCK SIZE: 2"

cut 2⅞" squares for half-squares

border #1: 1", cut 1½" strips

border #2: 1" pieced, cut 1½" squares

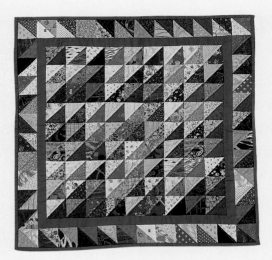

Scrappy Squares

by Mary Sowell

Create a scrappy look by using half-squares in a straight set. Add two borders, a narrow plain border strip and half-squares larger than those used in the center of the quilt.

BLOCK STYLE: Half-squares

FINISHED BLOCK SIZE: 2"

cut 2⅞" squares for half-squares

border #1: ¾", cut 1¼" strips

border #2: 2" pieced, cut 2⅞" squares for half-squares

Zigzag

by Mary Tharp

This layout is a good way to use charm exchange squares. Arrange half-squares in rows forming zigzags. Mary Tharp tied this quilt for a quick lap robe.

BLOCK STYLE: Half-squares

FINISHED BLOCK SIZE: 5⅛"

cut 6" squares for half-squares

Bordeaux

by Mary Sowell

Purples, greens, browns, and neutrals create this quilt of grapes hanging on the vine.

BLOCK STYLE: Half-squares

FINISHED BLOCK SIZE: ⅞"

cut 1½" squares for half-squares

border #1: ¾", cut 1¼" strips

border #2: 1½", cut 2" strips

Color Fun

by Mary Sowell

Shading the colors from lights to darks, corner to corner, adds interest to this straight-set quilt. The colors are carried out into the borders.

Block style: Half-squares

Finished block size: 2½"

cut 3⅜" squares for half-squares

borders: 2½", cut 3" strips

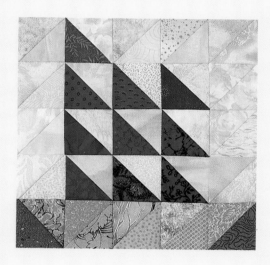

Sailboat

Use one key color for the sailboat, with light half-squares in the background.

Block style: 5-patch

Finished block size: 10"

cut 2⅞" squares for half-squares

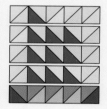

Tulip

Use a flower fabric with green leaves and background to create this Tulip block.

Block style: 9-patch

Finished block size: 6"

cut 2⅞" squares for half-squares

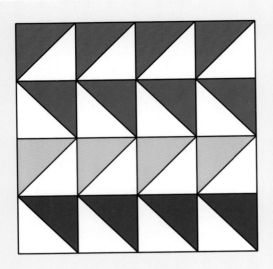

Hopscotch

Use four fabrics plus the background to create this graphic design.

BLOCK STYLE: 4-patch

FINISHED BLOCK SIZE: 8"

cut 2⅞" squares for half-squares

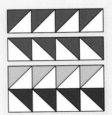

Pinwheel Star

A monochromatic color scheme, using light, medium, and dark fabrics is a good choice for this block.

BLOCK STYLE: 4-patch

FINISHED BLOCK SIZE: 8"

cut 2⅞" squares for half-squares

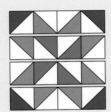

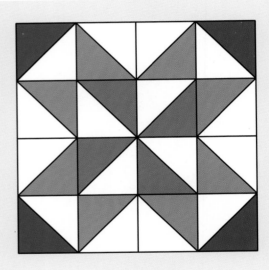

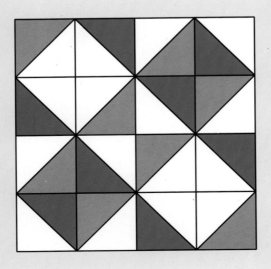

Triangle Beauty

Using three colors gives a positive-negative image to this block.

BLOCK STYLE: 4-patch

FINISHED BLOCK SIZE: 8"

cut 2⅞" squares for half-squares

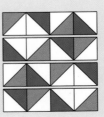

Hovering Hawks

Use several prints for the hawks and a blue background to depict the hawks hovering in the sky.

BLOCK STYLE: 9-patch

FINISHED BLOCK SIZE: 9"

cut 3⅞" squares to make the half-squares

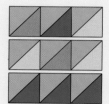

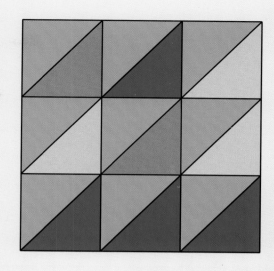

Broken Dishes

This design makes a good scrap quilt, with a variety of fabrics representing the fragments of broken dishes.

BLOCK STYLE: 4-patch

FINISHED BLOCK SIZE: 8"

cut 2⅞" squares to make the half-squares

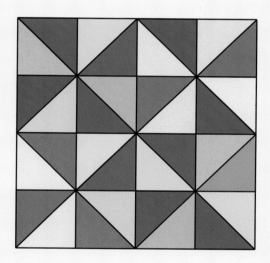

Sawtooth Star

Make a two-color quilt using light, medium, and dark fabrics.

BLOCK STYLE: 4-patch

FINISHED BLOCK SIZE: 12"

cut 3⅞" squares to make the half-squares

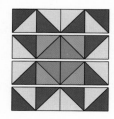

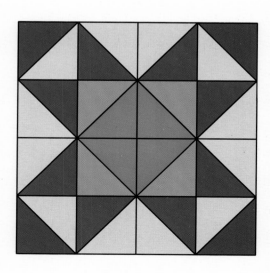

Maple Leaf

by Javada Smith

Fall colors add drama to this Maple Leaf block.

BLOCK STYLE: 9-patch

FINISHED BLOCK SIZE: 12"

cut 3⅞" squares for half-squares

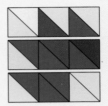

CORNER-SQUARE BLOCKS

Robbing Peter to Pay Paul

The triangles for this block are one division of a block, i.e., ¼ of a 4-patch or ⅓ of a 9-patch. Sew light 2½" squares in two corners of dark 6½" squares and dark 2½" squares in two corners of light 6½" squares to make positive/negative blocks. To assemble, alternate the light and dark blocks.

BLOCK STYLE: 9-patch

FINISHED BLOCK SIZE: 6"

cut 6½" large squares
cut 2½" small squares

Snowball

by Phyllis Miller

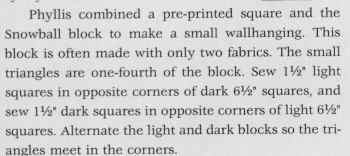

Phyllis combined a pre-printed square and the Snowball block to make a small wallhanging. This block is often made with only two fabrics. The small triangles are one-fourth of the block. Sew 1½" light squares in opposite corners of dark 6½" squares, and sew 1½" dark squares in opposite corners of light 6½" squares. Alternate the light and dark blocks so the triangles meet in the corners.

BLOCK STYLE: 4-patch

FINISHED BLOCK SIZE: Four pieced squares = 6" block

Kansas Dugout

Sew white 2" squares in opposite corners of print 3½" squares. Set the squares together with four white triangles meeting to form an on-point white square in the middle.

BLOCK STYLE: 4-patch

FINISHED BLOCK SIZE: 6"
    cut 3½" large squares
    cut 2" small squares

Lattice

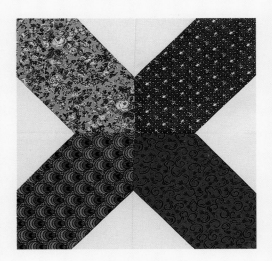

Sew white 2" squares in opposite corners of print 3½" squares, just like Kansas Dugout. Set the blocks together with the print corners meeting in the center.

BLOCK STYLE: 4-patch

FINISHED BLOCK SIZE: 6" block
    cut 3½" large squares
    cut 2" small squares

Bow Tie

Stitch a 1½" corner-square to one corner of two background squares. Set the squares together with the triangles meeting in the center. Alternate the Bow Ties with plain 4½" background blocks. If using a scrap look, you should have two squares from the same print to meet in the center of the block.

BLOCK STYLE: 4-patch

FINISHED BLOCK SIZE: 4"
    cut 2½" background squares
    cut 1½" squares for bow tie
    cut 2½" squares same as small
       bow tie squares

TRIANGLES COMBINED WITH SQUARES

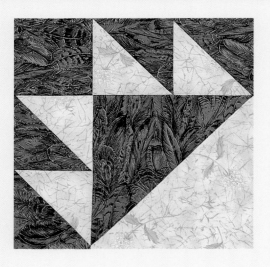

Sawtooth

Use two colors to create a variety of designs with this Sawtooth block. Play with these blocks to see what secondary designs appear. For a 6" block, cut 2⅞" squares to make the small half-squares; cut 4⅞" squares to make the large half-square. The plain square is cut 2½".

BLOCK STYLE: 9-patch
FINISHED BLOCK SIZE: 6"

9-Patch Star

Two fabrics and a background create this shining star.

BLOCK STYLE: 9-patch
FINISHED BLOCK SIZE: 9"

cut 3⅞" squares for half-squares
3" center square, cut 3½"

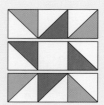

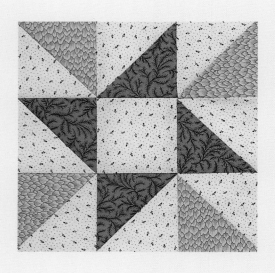

Ribbons & Stars

by Sue Rivers

Careful placement of fabrics from block to block helps to create the ribbons that run through this quilt. Two additional rows have been added around the center of the quilt to extend the ribbons to the borders.

BLOCK STYLE: 9-patch
FINISHED BLOCK SIZE: 2"

cut 2⅞" squares for half-squares
cut 2½" squares for plain squares
border #1: 2" green, cut 2½"
border #2: pieced, cut squares same as center
border #3: 3" green, cut 3½"

My Stars

by Sue Rivers

The four-pointed Friendship Star glows with 9" large stars and 3" small stars. Lay out blocks to keep the ribbon flowing across the quilt.

BLOCK STYLE: 9-patch

FINISHED BLOCK SIZE: 6"

cut 3⅞" squares for half-squares to make the large stars and ribbons

cut 1⅞" squares for half-squares to make the small stars, cut 1½" squares for the corner

border #1: 1½", cut 2"

border #2: ½", cut 1"

border #3: 2½", cut 3"

Wedding Ring

Create the illusion of a diamond wedding ring by using light, medium, and dark values.

BLOCK STYLE: 5-patch

FINISHED BLOCK SIZE: 10"

cut 2⅞" squares to make the half-squares

cut 2½" plain squares

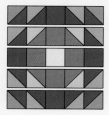

Hen & Chicks

Compare this design to Wedding Ring. It is exactly the same layout with different fabrics.

BLOCK STYLE: 5-patch

FINISHED BLOCK SIZE: 10"

cut 2⅞" squares to make the half-squares

cut 2½" plain squares

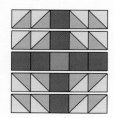

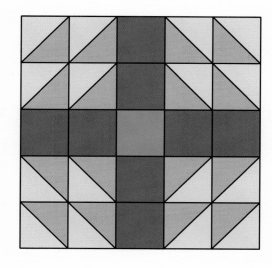

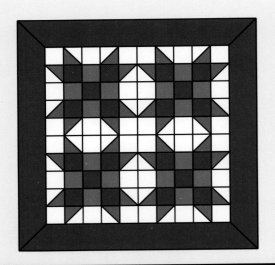

Checkered Star

See the Nine-patch in the center of this 5-patch star. Sew the Nine-patch by cutting strips 2½" wide; sew them in units of blue/red/blue and red/blue/red. Cut two blue/red/blue strips and one red/blue/red 2½" section for each block.

BLOCK STYLE: 5-patch

FINISHED BLOCK SIZE: 10"

cut 2⅞" squares to make the half-squares

cut plain 2½" plain squares of background

TWO SIZES OF TRIANGLES

Birds in the Air

Small half-squares make this a fun graphic design; try different settings to see how many variations you can make.

BLOCK STYLE: 9-patch

FINISHED BLOCK SIZE: 6"

cut 2⅞" squares for the small half-squares and three individual triangles

cut a 6⅞" square in half to make the large triangle.

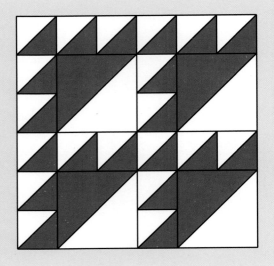

Barrister's Block

One large half-square is surrounded on two sides by small half-squares. Experiment with the setting to see how many different designs you can make with this block.

BLOCK STYLE: 9-patch

FINISHED BLOCK SIZE: 6"

cut 2⅞" squares for small half-squares

cut 4⅞" squares for large half-square

PLAY WITH TRIANGLES – Bonnie K. Browning & Phyllis D. Miller

Double T

This design is often seen in two colors. Play with the setting to see the variety of designs you can make with this block.

BLOCK STYLE: 9-patch

FINISHED BLOCK SIZE: 9"

cut 3⅞" squares for small half-squares

cut 6⅞" squares for the large half-square

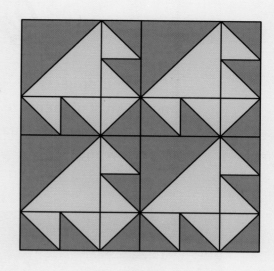

Album Block

Combine large and small half-squares to make this block. Pinwheels float across the surface of a quilt using this block.

BLOCK STYLE: 4-patch

FINISHED BLOCK SIZE: 8"

cut 2⅞" squares for small half-squares

cut 4⅞" squares for large half-squares

Pine Tree

Using half-squares makes this popular design easy to make. The grid method with two fabrics, green and white, is a real time saver for making a quilt with this design. Play with the layout of the blocks to create interesting secondary designs. Draw a horizontal and vertical grid with lines 2⅞" apart on the wrong side of the light fabric (see page 6).

BLOCK STYLE: 5-patch

FINISHED BLOCK SIZE: 10"

Projects

Several projects are included for you to begin playing with triangles. Most of them are scrap quilts so fabric yardage has not been calculated. Use the Squares from Yardage chart on page 9 to determine how much fabric you need.

Shades of Purple

by Marie Salazar

Finished quilt size: 31" x 38"
    6 blocks x 8 blocks
Finished block size: $4\frac{1}{8}$"
Border: $2\frac{3}{4}$", cut $3\frac{1}{4}$"

Make 24 half-squares, using one dark fabric and 6 values of purples. Cut 5" squares in the purple fabrics for a total 12; if you look at the photograph, you can see there are 6 triangles of some values and only two of others. Cut 12 squares of background. Sew the half-squares. Cut 24 additional $4\frac{5}{8}$" squares of background for the alternating blocks. Lay out the half-squares and background squares, arranging the purples from light to dark.

Cut $3\frac{1}{4}$" strips for the borders and sew to the edges, mitering the corners.

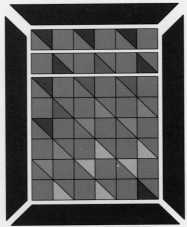

Quilt assembly

Floating Stars

by Phyllis Miller

FINISHED QUILT SIZE: 31" x 35"
    6 blocks x 7 blocks
FINISHED BLOCK SIZE: 4" finished
BORDER: 3", cut 3½"

Cut 42 – 4½" squares from background fabric. Cut 82 – 2½" scrap squares for the corners. Sew the small squares on opposite corners of the background squares to make 42 corner-square blocks (see p. 7). Lay out the blocks in a straight set to create the floating stars.

Cut 3½" wide strips for the borders from a striped fabric and sew to the edges of the quilt. Miter the corners.

This design can be made in any size. To find the size of the small square, divide the size of the finished block in half and add ½" for seam allowances.

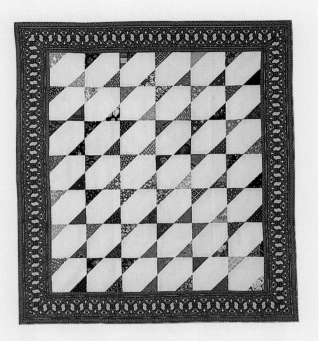

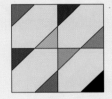

Quilt assembly

Judy's Xquisite Scrap Quilt

by Judy L. Hobbs

quilt made in a workshop with Bonnie Browning.

This scrap quilt is made from 9-patch blocks, using half-square triangles. The block is light on one half and dark on the other. Use this block in any design that can be used for a Log Cabin block. All these block arrangements — barn raising, flying geese, shaded flying geese, light and dark squares, positive/negative, and zigzag — are made by turning the half light/half dark blocks. Judy Hobbs' quilt is made by using an asymmetrical arrangement of the blocks.

barn raising

flying geese

shaded flying geese

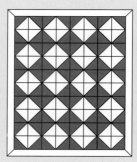

light and dark squares

positive/negative

zigzag

Examples using half light and half dark blocks

FINISHED QUILT SIZE: 54" x 81"
  without borders
BLOCK STYLE: 9-patch
FINISHED BLOCK SIZE: 9"
TO MAKE THE BLOCK, YOU NEED:
  3 light (L)/medium (M) half-squares
  3 light /dark (D) half-squares
  3 medium/dark half-squares

Make the blocks using the square method for the half-squares. Sort 3⅞" squares into light, medium, and dark piles. Draw a diagonal line from corner to corner on the light and medium squares as described on page 6. Sew three sets of L/M squares, three sets of L/D squares, and three sets of M/D using the chain piecing method (p. 8). Stitch on the left of the drawn line of all nine sets of squares, turn the strip around and sew on the opposite side of the line. Cut the squares apart, keeping the squares in order so you won't have to re-sort them. Cut on the drawn line. This will give you two identical half-squares. Sort them into piles to make laying out the blocks easier. Lay out each block as shown in the block assembly.

Assemble the half-squares in rows. Take care that you do not turn the half-squares or the rows as you sew them together. It may be helpful to pick up the half-square and immediately pin it to the edge of the next half-square. Sew all three rows to complete the block.

The fun part comes next. After you have made ten or twelve blocks, lay out the blocks by having the dark corners come together, by having the light corners come together, and by alternating light and dark corners. Once you have decided on a lay-out, sew the rows together and complete the quilt top. Because this quilt is scrappy, the borders can be kept simple to contain the motion of the quilt. Make a border using two or three strips in colors that dominate in the quilt.

This is a great quilt to send with your child to college or just to snuggle in.

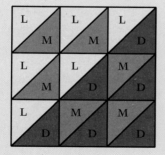

Block assembly

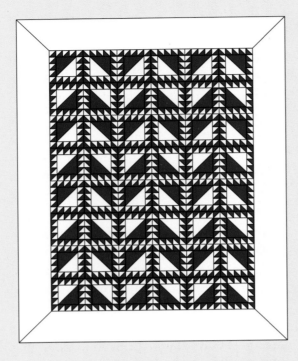

Lady of the Lake

This block makes a beautiful two-color quilt. It is often made in blues and white. You can use one blue and one white fabric or several values of each. The diagonal line of the large half-square gives a lot of motion to this quilt. Try different settings, ranging from the blocks set straight, or turn every other block to create the illusion of waves.

FINISHED QUILT SIZE: 80" x 100"
    6 blocks x 8 blocks
BLOCK STYLE: 5-patch
FINISHED BLOCK SIZE: 10"
BORDER: 10", cut 10½"

CUT FABRIC	MAKE 1 BLOCK	MAKE 48 BLOCKS FOR QUILT
2⅞" sq. blue	8	192
2⅞" sq. white	8	192
6⅞" sq. blue	1	24
6⅞" sq. white	1	24

Following the Block Assembly, sew five small half-squares together for the top row. Sew another set of five small half-squares for the bottom row. To make the sides, sew two sets of three small half-squares; sew one of these units on each side of the large half-square. Assemble the block. Make 48 blocks.

Sew eight rows of six blocks; assemble the quilt top.

Cut two 10½" x 82" and two 10½" x 102" strips for the borders. Sew the borders to the quilt, mitering the corners. A quilting design of cables or waves would be beautiful on this wide border.

Quilt assembly

Star in a Star

by Bonnie Browning

Make a patriotic star quilt using half-squares and squares.

FINISHED QUILT SIZE: 30" x 30"
FINISHED BLOCK SIZE: 12"
BORDER: 3", cut 3½"

CUT FABRIC	MAKE 1 BLOCK	MAKE 4 BLOCKS FOR QUILT
3½" sq. red	1	4
2⅛" sq. red	4	16
2⅛" sq. white	4	16
2" sq. white, corners	4	16
3⅞" sq. blue	4	16
3⅞" sq. white	4	16
3½" sq. white, corners	4	16

Sew four 2⅛" red and white squares to make eight half-squares. Make half-squares using the 3⅞" blue and white squares. Lay-out the block using the block assembly as a guide. Sew each row; stitch the rows together to complete each block.

To finish the quilt, sew four Star in a Star blocks. The border strips are cut 3½" x 31", two red and two blue. Sew the red borders to the quilt on two opposite sides; stitch the blue borders on the remaining two borders. Miter the corners.

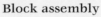

Block assembly

Quilt assembly

Southern Charm

by Phyllis D. Miller

Using the Flower Pot block, Phyllis Miller shows how you can change the design lines in a block and use many different fabrics to colorwash the quilt. The original block was changed to add lines to make the block of individual triangles.

This is a charm quilt, where every triangle is a different fabric. There are no repeats of fabric in the entire quilt. If you are trading fabric squares with friends, this quilt is a fun way to use some of those fabric pieces.

The triangles must be carefully chosen to give contrast between the flower pot design and the background. This quilt is unique because the background is entirely pieced of pastel fabrics. The pots are triangles in one color family and the flowers are in bright and dark colors.

Original Flower Pot block

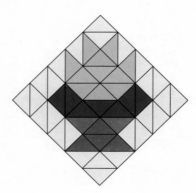

Phyllis's Southern Charm block

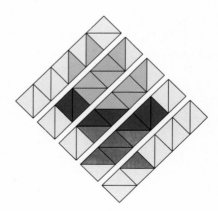

Block assembly

Quilt size: 47" x 47"

Finished Block style: 5-patch

Block size: 10"

Border: 2", cut 2⅞" square for individual triangles

Cut individual 2⅞" triangles; 26 lights, 6 of one color for the pot, and 18 brights and/or darks for the flowers are needed for each block. Lay out each block following the block assembly diagram. Thirteen blocks are needed to make the quilt. Sew each row; sew the rows together to complete the block.

The blocks are laid out on point; move them around until you are pleased with the design. Next, make the corner and side units to finish the rows.

Make four corner units using 24 individual triangles for each one; 96 light triangles are needed to make four corner units.

Eight side units, two on each side, are needed. For each block, cut 25 light triangles; use 200 individual triangles to make the eight side triangle units.

Sew the blocks in diagonal rows and stitch the rows together.

For the border, sew dark triangles together. The large triangles in the corners of the quilt are two 6⅛" squares cut in half diagonally.

Corner unit

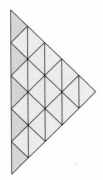

Side unit

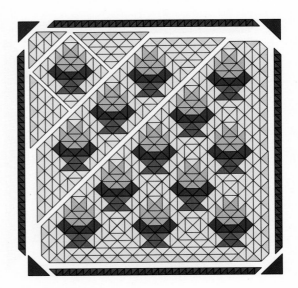

Quilt assembly

Jacob's Ladder

by Marie Salazar

This quilt combines half-squares with four-patches to make a 9-patch block. The placement of color and the layout create secondary designs in this quilt.

FINISHED QUILT SIZE: 41" x 41"
  4 blocks x 4 blocks
BLOCK STYLE: 9-patch
FINISHED BLOCK SIZE: 9"
BORDER: 2½", cut 3"

Cut 2" strips in two dark and two medium fabrics to make the five 4-patch units needed to make a block. To make 16 blocks, cut four strips each of four different fabrics.

To make the four half-squares needed for a block, cut 3⅞" squares. To make the quilt, you need to cut 32 light or medium squares and 32 dark squares. If you want high contrast, choose light squares or choose medium for a more muted effect.

Lay out each block; sew each row. Stitch the rows together to complete the block. Play with the blocks to explore the number of ways you can assemble them into a quilt.

Cut four strips, 3" x 42½", for borders. Sew the borders to the quilt and miter the corners.

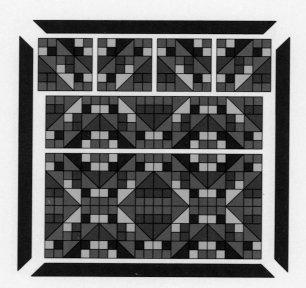

Quilt assembly

Bibliography

Brackman, Barbara. *Encyclopedia of Pieced Quilt Patterns*. Paducah, KY: American Quilter's Society, 1993.

Malone, Maggie. *1001 Patchwork Designs*. New York, NY: Sterling Publishing Company, Inc., 1982.

About the Authors

Authors Bonnie Browning and Phyllis Miller are active quilting instructors, who met in 1992 while serving on the Board of the National Quilting Association. Today, they live just 35 miles apart and spend a lot of time visiting and quilting together.

Bonnie K. Browning began quilting in 1979, and started teaching quilt-making in 1985. She travels to teach quilting at conferences throughout the U.S., Australia, and Turkey. Bonnie is a certified judge and is qualified to judge master quilts. Her quilts have won awards at the local, state, and national levels.

Books written by Bonnie include *Paper Pieced Patterns*, AQS, 1999; *Flowering Dogwood Patterns*, AQS, 1998; *Borders & Finishing Touches*, AQS, 1997; and *Ribbons & Threads: Baltimore Style*, AQS, 1996. *Any Body Can Learn to Quilt* is scheduled to be released in the fall of 2000.

Phyllis D. Miller began quilting in the summer of 1968, and teaches and judges quiltmaking for guilds and conferences across the U.S. She makes both traditional and innovative quilts, often combining both ideas in one piece. Her quilts have been exhibited and won awards in local, state, and national shows.

Her first book, *Encyclopedia of Designs for Quilting*, was published by the American Quilter's Society in 1996, and her second, *Sets & Sashings*, will be released in the summer of 2000.

Other AQS Books

This is only a small selection of the books available from the American Quilter's Society. AQS books are known worldwide for timely topics, clear writing, beautiful color photos, and accurate illustrations and patterns. The following books are available from your local bookseller, quilt shop, or public library.

#5705 $22.95

#5642 $14.95

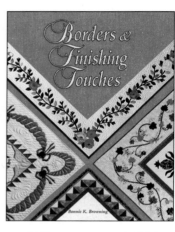

#4898 $16.95

#5140 $14.95

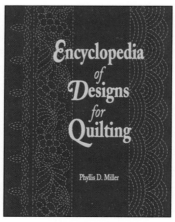

#4814 $34.95

#5590 $24.95